foreword

Anyone lucky enough to coax fresh strawberries from a garden or patio planter knows the thrill of finding that first late-spring berry, bursting with flavour and the promise of summer. All through July, August and into September, even non-gardeners can revel in the delights of this luscious fruit, piled high at farmers' markets and grocery stores. Shortcakes and salads and even strawberry wine help us celebrate the season.

And when cold winds blow, we can turn to our cache of easy jams and frozen berries to remind us of summer's delicious bounty. In this handy little book of strawberry recipes, collected from the best in the Company's Coming library, you'll find great ideas to celebrate this sweet fruit. Whether it's a chilled soup or a warm muffin, these are recipes to savour—each sip or bite will say "so strawberry"!

Jean Paré

double strawberry toast

Strawberries as far as the eye can see! These French toast sandwiches have strawberries inside and out. You can substitute regular milk for the soy milk.

Liquid honey	1/4 cup	60 mL
Lime juice	2 tbsp.	30 mL
Grated lime zest	1 tsp.	5 mL
Sliced fresh strawberries	3 cups	750 mL
Large eggs	4	4
Vanilla soy milk	1 cup	250 mL
Coconut (or vanilla) extract	1/2 tsp.	2 mL
Strawberry jam	2/3 cup	150 mL
Whole-grain bread slices	12	12
Cooking oil	2 tbsp.	30 mL

Combine first 3 ingredients in medium bowl. Add strawberries. Stir well. Set aside.

Whisk next 3 ingredients in large shallow bowl until frothy. Set aside.

Spread about 1 1/2 tbsp. (25 mL) jam on 1 bread slice. Cover with second bread slice. Repeat with remaining jam and bread slices, making 6 sandwiches.

Heat 1 tbsp. (15 mL) cooking oil in large frying pan on medium-low. Press one sandwich into egg mixture. Turn over to coat both sides. Transfer to frying pan. Repeat with 2 more sandwiches. Cook for about 4 minutes per side until golden. Transfer to serving platter. Keep warm in 200°F (95°C) oven. Repeat with remaining oil, sandwiches and egg mixture. Spoon about 1/2 cup (125 mL) strawberry mixture over each sandwich. Serves 6.

1 serving: 407 calories; 10.7 g Total Fat (4.9 g Mono, 2.5 g Poly, 1.9 g Sat); 124 mg Cholesterol; 69 g Carbohydrate; 5 g Fibre; 11 g Protein; 318 mg Sodium

christmas morning muesli

Make it a special holiday breakfast any time strawberries are at hand. Assemble this a day ahead to allow the granola to soften into a traditional muesli texture. A little granola sprinkled on top adds a satisfying crunch.

Granola	3 cups	750 mL
Fresh strawberries, halved lengthwise	1 lb.	454 g
Vanilla yogurt	3 cups	750 mL
Fresh (or frozen, thawed) blueberries	1 cup	250 mL
Kiwifruit, sliced	3	3
Can of mandarin orange segments, drained	10 oz.	284 mL
Fresh strawberries, halved lengthwise	6	6
Granola	1/2 cup	125 mL

Layer first 6 ingredients in large glass bowl as follows:

1. 1 1/2 cups (375 mL) granola
2. Some strawberry halves, pressed cut-side out against inside of bowl to decorate. Layer remaining strawberry halves on top of granola.
3. 1 cup (250 mL) yogurt
4. 1/2 cup (125 mL) blueberries
5. Remaining granola
6. Some kiwifruit slices, pressed cut-side out against inside of bowl to decorate. Layer remaining kiwifruit slices on top of granola.
7. 1 cup (250 mL) yogurt
8. Remaining blueberries
9. Remaining yogurt
10. Some orange segments, pressed against inside of bowl to decorate. Scatter remaining orange segments on top of yogurt.

Arrange second amount of strawberries over top. Chill, covered, for at least 6 hours or overnight.

Just before serving, sprinkle second amount of granola over top. Makes about 8 cups (2 L).

3/4 cup (175 mL): 314 Calories; 13.3 g Total Fat (3.7 g Mono, 6.1 g Poly, 2.9 g Sat); 4 mg Cholesterol; 45 g Carbohydrate; 5 g Fibre; 9 g Protein; 48 mg Sodium

berry bran shake

Breakfast in a glass! The natural sweetness of fruit gets a high-fibre boost from bran flakes to make a fast, delicious start to your day. Fresh strawberries can easily be substituted for the frozen.

Frozen whole strawberries, partially thawed and cut up	2 cups	500 mL
Milk	2 cups	500 mL
Raisin bran cereal	1/2 cup	125 mL
Chopped pitted dates	1/4 cup	60 mL

Process all 4 ingredients in blender or food processor until smooth. Makes about 4 cups (1 L).

1 cup: 132 Calories; 1.8 g Total Fat (0.4 g Mono, 0.2 g Poly, 0.9 g Sat); 5 mg Cholesterol; 26 g Carbohydrate; 4 g Fibre; 5 g Protein; 109 mg Sodium

soy-slim shake

If you've got a bumper crop of berries, go ahead and add a few more to the blender. It's easy to substitute other fruit too. The ice makes the soy milk separate, but the combination of flavours is fabulous.

Soy (or skim) milk	2 cups	500 mL
Medium banana, cut up	1	1
Crushed ice	1 cup	250 mL
Sliced fresh (or frozen, thawed) strawberries	1 cup	250 mL
Liquid honey	1 tbsp.	15 mL

Process all 5 ingredients in blender or food processor until smooth. Makes about 4 cups (1 L).

1 cup (250 mL): 98 Calories; 2.7 g Total Fat (0.5 g Mono, 1.2 g Poly, 0.3 g Sat); 0 mg Cholesterol; 16 g Carbohydrate; 2 g Fibre; 4 g Protein; 16 mg Sodium

strawberry wine

Choose a wine without bubbles, as they'll disappear before you get to taste it. Once it's finished, its sweetness rating is about a two or three.

Dry (or alcohol-free) white wine	3 cups	750 mL
Granulated sugar	1/4 cup	60 mL
Sliced fresh strawberries	2 cups	500 mL

Measure wine and sugar into pitcher or medium bowl. Stir until sugar is dissolved.

Add strawberries. Stir. Chill, covered, for 3 days to blend flavours. Strain through fine sieve into jar with tight-fitting lid. Discard solids. Store in refrigerator for up to 2 weeks. Makes about 3 cups (750 mL).

1/2 cup (125 mL): 129 Calories; 0.2 g Total Fat (trace Mono, 0.1 Poly, trace Sat); 0 mg Cholesterol; 13 g Carbohydrate; 1 g Fibre; trace Protein; 7 mg Sodium

strawberry soup

Chill your bowls, or even wide-rimmed champagne glasses, before serving this refreshing soup.

Water	1 1/2 cups	375 mL
Granulated sugar	3/4 cup	175 mL
Fresh strawberries, halved	4 cups	1 L
Sweet sherry (or orange juice)	1/4 cup	60 mL
Grated orange zest	2 tsp.	10 mL
Grated lemon zest	1 1/2 tsp.	7 mL
Whipping cream (optional)	4 tsp.	20 mL

Combine water and sugar in small saucepan. Bring to a boil, stirring occasionally. Reduce heat to medium-low. Simmer, uncovered, for 10 minutes. Cool to room temperature.

Combine next 4 ingredients in large bowl. Add sugar mixture. Stir. Process in 2 batches in blender until smooth. Strain juice into medium bowl. Discard seeds. Chill, covered, for at least 2 hours until cold.

Drizzle individual servings with whipping cream. Makes about 3 1/2 cups (875 mL). Serves 4.

1 serving: 212 Calories; 0.6 g Total Fat (trace Mono, 0.3 g Poly, trace Sat); 0 mg Cholesterol; 51 g Carbohydrate; 4 g Fibre; 1 g Protein; 3 mg Sodium

spring salad

Fresh spinach and strawberries—summer's just around the corner!

| Fresh spinach leaves, lightly packed | 6 cups | 1.5 L |
| Fresh strawberries, halved | 2 cups | 500 mL |

SWEET AND SOUR DRESSING		
Granulated sugar	1/4 cup	60 mL
Apple cider vinegar	3 tbsp.	50 mL
Sesame seeds, toasted (see Tip, page 64)	1 1/2 tbsp.	25 mL
Poppy seeds	2 tsp.	10 mL
Onion powder	1/4 tsp.	1 mL
Worcestershire sauce	1/4 tsp.	1 mL

Put spinach and strawberries into large bowl. Toss.

Sweet and Sour Dressing: Process all 6 ingredients in blender until smooth. Makes about 1/3 cup (75 mL) dressing. Drizzle over spinach mixture. Toss. Serves 6.

1 serving: 84 Calories; 2.1 g Total Fat (0.6 g Mono, 1.0 g Poly, 0.3 g Sat); 0 mg Cholesterol; 16 g Carbohydrate; 3 g Fibre; 2 g Protein; 42 mg Sodium

strawberry pecan salad

Warming up the strawberry jam infuses the dressing with a wonderful berry flavour.

Pecan pieces	2/3 cup	150 mL
Granulated sugar	1/2 cup	125 mL
Water	1/4 cup	60 mL
Fresh spinach leaves, lightly packed	6 cups	1.5 L
Sliced fresh strawberries	2 cups	500 mL
Goat (chèvre) cheese, cut up (optional)	3 oz.	85 g
STRAWBERRY DRESSING		
Olive (or cooking) oil	3 tbsp.	50 mL
Balsamic vinegar	2 tbsp.	30 mL
Strawberry jam, warmed	2 tbsp.	30 mL
Pepper	1/8 tsp.	0.5 mL

Spread pecans evenly on ungreased baking sheet with sides. Bake in 350°F (175°C) oven for 5 to 10 minutes, stirring or shaking often, until golden.

Combine sugar and water in small saucepan on low. Heat and stir until sugar is dissolved. Bring to a boil on medium-high. Boil, uncovered, for 5 to 10 minutes, without stirring, until golden. Drizzle over pecans. Let stand for about 20 minutes until cool and hard. Chop.

Arrange spinach on 6 salad plates. Scatter pecans, strawberries and cheese over top.

Strawberry Dressing: Combine all 4 ingredients in jar with tight-fitting lid. Shake well. Makes about 1/2 cup (125 mL) dressing. Drizzle over each salad. Serves 6.

1 serving: 269 Calories; 16.7 g Total Fat (9.9 g Mono, 4.6 g Poly, 1.3 g Sat); 0 mg Cholesterol; 31 g Carbohydrate; 4 g Fibre; 3 g Protein; 50 mg Sodium

pineapple boat salad

Pineapples don't continue to ripen once they're picked, so choose a sweet-smelling one with fresh, green leaves and no soft spots.

Fresh pineapple (leaves attached), halved lengthwise	1	1
Halved fresh strawberries	1 cup	250 mL
Halved seedless green (or red) grapes	1/2 cup	125 mL
Medium banana, sliced	1	1
Kiwifruit, sliced	1	1
1% cottage cheese	1 cup	250 mL
Chopped pecans (or walnuts)	1/4 cup	60 mL
Chopped green onion	1 tbsp.	15 mL
Chopped pecans (or walnuts), for garnish		

Remove and discard core from pineapple halves. Cut out pineapple, leaving 1/2 inch (12 mm) shell. Cut pineapple into bite-sized pieces. Place in medium bowl.

Add next 4 ingredients. Toss gently. Spoon into pineapple halves.

Combine next 3 ingredients in small bowl. Spoon onto fruit mixture.

Garnish with pecans. Serves 4.

1 serving: 221 Calories; 6.9 g Total Fat (3.6 g Mono, 1.6 g Poly, 0.9 g Sat); 3 mg Cholesterol; 34 g Carbohydrate; 4 g Fibre; 10 g Protein; 253 mg Sodium

strawberry citrus salad

A hint of orange liqueur accents the pairing of strawberries and oranges. You can make this a few hours ahead, cover and refrigerate. Give it a gentle toss before serving.

Medium oranges	5	5
Quartered fresh strawberries	5 cups	1.25 L
Orange liqueur	1/4 cup	60 mL
Liquid honey	3 tbsp.	50 mL

Cut small slice of peel from both ends of each orange to expose flesh. Place oranges, cut-side down, on cutting board. Remove peel with sharp knife, cutting down and around flesh, leaving as little pith as possible (inset photo). Cut oranges in half lengthwise. Place each half cut-side down. Cut crosswise into 1/4 inch (6 mm) slices. Put into large bowl.

Add strawberries. Toss gently.

Combine liqueur and honey in small cup. Drizzle over fruit mixture. Toss gently. Serves 12.

1 serving: 75 Calories; 0.3 g Total Fat (0.1 g Mono, 0.2 g Poly, trace Sat); 0 mg Cholesterol; 16 g Carbohydrate; 3 g Fibre; 1 g Protein; 1 mg Sodium

strawberry muffins

Biscuit-textured muffins with bits of strawberry that explode in your mouth with every bite!

All-purpose flour	2 cups	500 mL
Baking powder	1 tbsp.	15 mL
Salt	1/2 tsp.	2 mL
Butter (or hard margarine), softened	1/4 cup	60 mL
Granulated sugar	1/2 cup	125 mL
Large egg	1	1
Vanilla extract	1/2 tsp.	2 mL
Chopped fresh (or frozen, thawed) strawberries	1 1/4 cups	300 mL
Strawberry yogurt (not non-fat)	1 cup	250 mL

Measure first 3 ingredients into large bowl. Stir. Make a well in centre. Set aside.

Cream butter and sugar in medium bowl. Add egg and vanilla. Beat well.

Add strawberries and yogurt. Stir well. Add to well in flour mixture. Stir until just moistened. Batter will be thick. Fill 12 greased muffin cups 3/4 full. Bake in 400°F (205°C) oven for about 20 minutes until wooden pick inserted in centre of muffin comes out clean. Let stand in pan for 5 minutes. Remove muffins from pan and place on wire rack to cool. Makes 12 muffins.

1 muffin: 188 Calories; 5.4 g Total Fat (1.5 g Mono, 0.4 g Poly, 3.1 g Sat); 31 mg Cholesterol; 31 g Carbohydrate; 1 g Fibre; 4 g Protein; 252 mg Sodium

strawberry loaf

Wrap individual slices and freeze for fast lunch-bag treats.

Mashed fresh (or frozen, thawed) strawberries	1 cup	250 mL
All-purpose flour	1 3/4 cups	425 mL
Baking soda	1 tsp.	5 mL
Salt	3/4 tsp.	4 mL
Baking powder	1/2 tsp.	2 mL
Ground cinnamon	1/2 tsp.	2 mL
Chopped walnuts (optional)	1/2 cup	125 mL
Hard margarine (or butter), softened	6 tbsp.	100 mL
Granulated sugar	1 cup	250 mL
Large eggs	2	2
Water	1/3 cup	75 mL
Vanilla extract	1/2 tsp.	2 mL

Put strawberries into small saucepan. Heat and stir on medium-high until boiling. Reduce heat to medium-low. Simmer, uncovered, for 1 minute, stirring often. Cool.

Measure next 6 ingredients into large bowl. Stir. Make a well in centre.

Cream margarine and sugar in large bowl. Add eggs, 1 at a time, beating well after each addition. Add water, vanilla and strawberries. Stir well. Add to well. Stir until just moistened. Spread in greased 9 x 5 x 3 inch (22 x 12.5 x 7.5 cm) loaf pan. Bake in 350°F (175°C) oven for 60 to 65 minutes until wooden pick inserted in centre comes out clean. Let stand in pan for 10 minutes. Remove loaf from pan and place on wire rack to cool. Cuts into 18 slices.

1 slice: 139 Calories; 4.6 g Total Fat (2.8 g Mono, 0.5 g Poly, 1.0 g Sat); 24 mg Cholesterol; 22 g Carbohydrate; 1 g Fibre; 2 g Protein; 233 mg Sodium

strawberry cream cookies

Bring out some of that Freezer Strawberry Jam, page 32, for these buttery cookie sandwiches oozing with sweet, creamy filling.

Butter (or hard margarine), softened	3/4 cup	175 mL
Brown sugar, packed	1/2 cup	125 mL
Large egg	1	1
Vanilla extract	1/2 tsp.	2 mL
All-purpose flour	2 cups	500 mL
Medium unsweetened coconut	1/2 cup	125 mL
Baking powder	2 tsp.	10 mL
Baking soda	1/4 tsp.	1 mL
Salt	1/4 tsp.	1 mL
STRAWBERRY FILLING		
Butter (or hard margarine), softened	1/4 cup	60 mL
Icing (confectioner's) sugar	3/4 cup	175 mL
Strawberry jam	2 tbsp.	30 mL
Strawberry jam	1/3 cup	75 mL

Cream butter and brown sugar in large bowl. Add egg and vanilla. Beat well.

Combine next 5 ingredients in medium bowl. Add to butter mixture in 2 additions, mixing well after each addition until no dry flour remains. Roll into balls, using 2 tsp. (10 mL) for each. Arrange about 1 1/2 inches (3.8 cm) apart on greased cookie sheets. Flatten with fork to 1/4 inch (6 mm) thickness. Bake in 375°F (190°C) oven for 7 to 10 minutes until firm and edges are golden. Let stand on cookie sheets for 5 minutes. Remove cookies from cookie sheets and place on wire racks to cool. Makes about 56 cookies.

Strawberry Filling: Cream butter and icing sugar in small bowl. Add first amount of jam. Beat until smooth. Makes about 1/2 cup (125 mL) filling. Lay half of cookies, bottom-side up, on work surface. Spread each with about 1 tsp. (5 mL) filling.

Lay remaining cookies, bottom-side up, on work surface. Spread each with about 1/2 tsp. (2 mL) of second amount of jam. Sandwich cookies using 1 cookie with filling and 1 cookie with jam. Makes 28 sandwich cookies.

1 sandwich cookie: 152 Calories; 8.4 g Total Fat (2.1 g Mono, 0.3 g Poly, 5.4 g Sat); 27 mg Cholesterol; 19 g Carbohydrate; trace Fibre; 1 g Protein; 137 mg Sodium

strawberry flowers

So pretty! If you're pressed for time, forget about the filigree petals—just squeeze chocolate designs directly onto individual plates.

ALMOND CUSTARD FILLING

Granulated sugar	1/4 cup	60 mL
All-purpose flour	1 tbsp.	15 mL
Cornstarch	1 tbsp.	15 mL
Salt	1/16 tsp.	0.5 mL
Homogenized milk	3/4 cup	175 mL
Egg yolk (large)	1	1
Butter (or hard margarine)	1 tsp.	5 mL
Almond extract	1/2 tsp.	2 mL
Large fresh strawberries	12	12

CHOCOLATE FILIGREES

Semi-sweet chocolate chips	3/4 cup	175 mL

Almond Custard Filling: Combine first 4 ingredients in small heavy saucepan. Slowly stir in milk. Heat on medium for about 5 minutes, stirring constantly, until boiling and thickened. Remove from heat.

Beat egg yolk with fork in small cup. Add 2 tbsp. (30 mL) hot milk mixture. Stir well. Slowly add egg yolk mixture to hot milk mixture in saucepan. Cook on medium-low for about 1 minute, stirring constantly, until thickened. Remove from heat.

Stir in butter and extract. Cover with plastic wrap directly on surface to prevent skin from forming. Chill. Makes about 3/4 cup (175 mL) filling.

Slice hulls from strawberries, making flat base for strawberries to stand upright. Make 3 crosscuts (✳) from tip of each strawberry almost, but not quite through, to base. Carefully spread cuts open to make 6 "petals." Pipe about 1 tbsp. (15 mL) filling into centre of each strawberry (photo 1). Chill, covered.

Chocolate Filigrees: Heat chocolate chips in small heavy saucepan on lowest heat, stirring often, until almost melted. Do not overheat. Remove from heat. Stir until smooth.

Spoon about 1/4 of melted chocolate into piping bag fitted with smallest plain tip or small resealable freezer bag with tiny piece snipped off corner. Pipe into 9 medium-sized petal outlines on narrow strip of waxed paper (photo 2). Immediately lay over rolling pin or other curved object. If filigrees will not fall into curve, warm with hair dryer. Chill for 10 minutes before carefully removing from rolling pin. Peel off paper. Transfer filigrees to plates. Repeat with remaining melted chocolate, for a total of 36 petals, rewarming chocolate on low as necessary.

Arrange 3 strawberries on each of 4 plates. Arrange 9 petals around strawberries on each plate. Use small dabs of chocolate to anchor petals and strawberries onto plates (photo 3). Chill for up to 2 hours until ready to serve. Serves 4.

1 serving: 298 Calories; 14.1 g Total Fat (4.6 g Mono, 0.7 g Poly, 7.9 g Sat); 63 mg Cholesterol; 44 g Carbohydrate; 3 g Fibre; 4 g Protein; 79 mg Sodium

chocolate nut strawberries

Sweet, juicy strawberries dipped in chocolate and coated with almonds.
Divinely decadent! For a variation, try white chocolate squares.

Semi-sweet chocolate baking squares **(1 oz., 28 g, each), chopped**	4	4
Large fresh strawberries **(with stems), blotted dry**	12	12
Finely chopped natural almonds, **toasted (see Tip, page 64)**	1/2 cup	125 mL

Heat chocolate in small heavy saucepan on lowest heat, stirring often, until chocolate is almost melted. Do not overheat. Remove from heat. Stir until smooth. Pour chocolate into small bowl.

Holding 1 strawberry by stem end, dip straight down into chocolate until 2/3 of the way up strawberry.

Immediately roll strawberry in almonds in small shallow dish until coated. Place on waxed paper-lined baking sheet. Repeat with remaining strawberries, chocolate and almonds. Chill until chocolate is set. Makes 12 strawberries.

1 strawberry: 84 Calories; 5.9 g Total Fat (2.9 g Mono, 0.8 g Poly, 1.9 g Sat); 0 mg Cholesterol; 8 g Carbohydrate; 1 g Fibre; 2 g Protein; 2 mg Sodium

freezer strawberry jam

What an easy way to guarantee fresh strawberry flavour throughout the year!

Granulated sugar	5 cups	1.25 L
Mashed fresh (or frozen, thawed) strawberries	3 cups	750 mL
Water	1 cup	250 mL
Pectin crystals	2 oz.	57 g

Combine sugar and strawberries in large bowl. Let stand for 10 minutes.

Combine water and pectin crystals in small saucepan. Heat and stir until boiling. Boil for 1 minute, stirring constantly. Remove from heat. Pour over strawberries. Stir for 2 minutes. Fill sterile freezer containers, leaving about 1 inch (2.5 cm) space at top. Let stand at room temperature for 24 hours until set. Store in freezer for up to 12 months. Refrigerate after opening. Makes about 7 cups (1.75 L).

1 tbsp. (15 mL): 34 Calories; trace Total Fat (0 g Mono, trace Poly, 0 g Sat); 0 mg Cholesterol; 9 g Carbohydrate; trace Fibre; trace Protein; 1 mg Sodium

strawberry parfait

In this easy, elegant-looking dessert you can substitute two cups of whipped cream for the envelope of dessert topping.

Envelope of dessert topping (prepared)	1	1
Can of crushed pineapple, well drained	14 oz.	398 mL
Granulated sugar	3 tbsp.	50 mL
Almond extract	1/4 tsp.	1 mL
Container of frozen strawberries in light syrup, thawed	15 oz.	425 g
Grenadine syrup (or 2 tbsp., 30 mL, granulated sugar)	2 tbsp.	30 mL
Maraschino cherries	6	6

Combine first 4 ingredients in medium bowl.

Combine strawberries with syrup and grenadine in separate medium bowl. Spoon 1/3 of pineapple mixture into 6 parfait or medium glasses. Spoon half of strawberry mixture on top. Repeat layers with remaining pineapple mixture and strawberry mixture, ending with pineapple mixture.

Top with cherries. Chill. Makes 6 parfaits.

1 parfait: 193 Calories; 3.7 g Total Fat (0.3 g Mono, 0.1 g Poly, 3.0 g Sat); 2.8 mg Cholesterol; 42 g Carbohydrate; 2 g Fibre; 2 g Protein; 30 mg Sodium

strawberry cream layers

For a special touch, drizzle plates with melted chocolate and pink chocolate melting wafers before placing the dessert on top.

Package of puff pastry (14 oz., 397 g), thawed according to package directions	1/2	1/2
FRESH STRAWBERRY FILLING		
Chopped fresh strawberries	1 1/2 cups	375 mL
Strawberry jam, warmed	1/3 cup	75 mL
Icing (confectioner's) sugar	1/4 cup	60 mL
Orange liqueur	1 tbsp.	15 mL
Whipping cream	1 cup	250 mL
Icing (confectioner's) sugar, for garnish		
Fresh strawberries, halved, for garnish		

Roll out puff pastry on lightly floured surface to 12 inch (30 cm) square. Place on greased baking sheet. Grease bottom of a second baking sheet. Place on top of pastry. Bake in 450°F (230°C) oven for 15 to 20 minutes until golden. Remove pastry from baking sheet and place on wire rack to cool. Cut into 12 rectangles.

Fresh Strawberry Filling: Combine first 4 ingredients in large bowl. Chill, covered, for 30 minutes to blend flavours. Drain, reserving syrup to drizzle on plates.

Beat whipping cream in medium bowl until soft peaks form. Fold into strawberry mixture. Makes about 3 cups (750 mL) filling. Spread 6 tbsp. (100 mL) filling on 1 pastry rectangle. Place second pastry rectangle on top. Spread with another 6 tbsp. (100 mL) filling. Top with third pastry rectangle. Repeat with remaining pastry rectangles and filling, making 4 individual desserts.

Sprinkle with icing sugar. Garnish with strawberries. Serves 4.

1 serving: 591 Calories; 39.4 g Total Fat (10.3 g Mono, 11.6 g Poly, 15.3 g Sat); 73 mg Cholesterol; 55 g Carbohydrate; 2 g Fibre; 6 g Protein; 158 mg Sodium

strawberries and cream

Rich and wonderful without being too sweet.

Water	1 1/2 cups	375 mL
Can of sweetened condensed milk	11 oz.	300 mL
Box of instant vanilla pudding powder (4-serving size)	1	1
Frozen whipped topping, thawed	4 cups	1 L
Frozen pound cake, thawed, cut into 1/2 inch (12 mm) cubes	10 1/2 oz.	298 g
Sliced fresh strawberries	4 cups	1 L
Slivered almonds, toasted (see Tip, page 64)	1/4 cup	60 mL

Beat water and condensed milk in medium bowl until well combined. Add pudding powder. Beat until smooth. Chill, uncovered, for about 5 minutes until set. Stir.

Fold whipped topping into pudding mixture.

Spread 2 cups (500 mL) pudding mixture into large glass bowl. Scatter half of cake cubes and half of strawberries over pudding mixture. Layer half of remaining pudding mixture, remaining cake and strawberries, in order given, over strawberries. Spoon remaining pudding mixture over top.

Sprinkle with almonds. Serves 12.

1 serving: 355 Calories; 15.7 g Total Fat (4.3 g Mono, 1.5 g Poly, 9.0 g Sat); 49 mg Cholesterol; 50 g Carbohydrate; 1 g Fibre; 5 g Protein; 120 mg Sodium

dessert special

You may have to put a burglar alarm on your fridge after you've made this. Family members have been known to sneak spoonfuls before company arrives!

Hard margarine (or butter)	1/2 cup	125 mL
Finely crushed vanilla wafers (about 52 wafers)	2 cups	500 mL
Block of light cream cheese, softened	8 oz.	250 g
Hard margarine (or butter), softened	1/2 cup	125 mL
Icing (confectioner's) sugar	1 1/2 cups	375 mL
Container of frozen strawberries in light syrup, thawed and drained	15 oz.	425 g
Can of crushed pineapple, drained	14 oz.	398 mL
Frozen whipped topping, thawed	4 cups	1 L
Sliced almonds, toasted (see Tip, page 64)	1/2 cup	125 mL

Melt first amount of margarine in small saucepan on medium. Remove from heat. Add wafer crumbs. Mix well. Press firmly into ungreased 9 x 13 inch (22 x 33 cm) pan. Bake in 350°F (175°C) oven for 8 to 10 minutes until golden. Let stand in pan on wire rack until cooled completely.

Mash cream cheese and second amount of margarine with fork in medium bowl. Add icing sugar. Beat until well combined. Spread evenly over crust.

Combine strawberries and pineapple in small bowl. Scatter over cream cheese mixture.

Spread with whipped topping. Sprinkle with almonds. Chill for at least 4 hours until set. Cuts into 18 pieces.

1 piece: 311 Calories; 20.6 g Total Fat (9.7 g Mono, 2.0 g Poly, 7.9 g Sat); 12.8 mg Cholesterol; 31 g Carbohydrate; trace Fibre; 3 g Protein; 289 mg Sodium

strawberry shortcakes

If ever there was a dessert that says "strawberry," this is it. The hint of cinnamon updates this classic recipe.

All-purpose flour	2 cups	500 mL
Granulated sugar	2 tbsp.	30 mL
Baking powder	1 tbsp.	15 mL
Salt	1/8 tsp.	0.5 mL
Hard margarine (or butter), cut up	2 tbsp.	30 mL
Buttermilk (or soured milk, see Tip, page 64)	1 cup	250 mL
Sliced fresh strawberries	4 cups	1 L
Granulated sugar	1/3 cup	75 mL
Orange liqueur	2 tbsp.	30 mL
Whipping cream	1 cup	250 mL
Granulated sugar	1 tbsp.	15 mL
Ground cinnamon	1/4 tsp.	1 mL

Combine first 4 ingredients in large bowl. Cut in margarine until mixture resembles coarse crumbs. Make a well in centre.

Add buttermilk to well. Stir until soft dough forms. Turn out onto lightly floured surface. Knead 8 times. Roll out or pat dough to about 3/4 inch (2 cm) thickness. Cut out 6 circles with lightly floured 2 3/4 inch (7 cm) cookie cutter. Arrange, almost touching, in lightly greased 9 x 9 inch (22 x 22 cm) pan. Bake in 450°F (230°C) oven for 12 to 15 minutes until lightly golden. Let stand in pan for 5 minutes. Remove biscuits from pan and place on wire rack to cool.

Combine next 3 ingredients in medium bowl. Chill.

Beat whipping cream in small bowl until soft peaks form. Add sugar and cinnamon. Stir. Cut shortcakes in half horizontally. Spread about 1/4 cup (60 mL) whipped cream mixture and about 1/2 cup (125 mL) strawberry mixture on bottom half of each shortcake. Cover with top halves. Makes 6 shortcakes.

1 shortcake: 466 Calories; 18.6 g Total Fat (6.7 g Mono, 1.2 g Poly, 9.5 g Sat); 50 mg Cholesterol; 66 g Carbohydrate; 4 g Fibre; 8 g Protein; 345 mg Sodium

chocolate layered cake

Amaretti *is the Italian name for macaroons. Crisp and crunchy on the outside and soft on the inside, these cookies, and their crumbs, are perfect for absorbing the orange liqueur. If your grocer doesn't carry them, try an Italian food store.*

Package of amaretti cookies	7.1 oz.	200 g
Orange liqueur	1/4 cup	60 mL
Dark chocolate bars (3 1/2 oz., 100 g, each), chopped	5	5
Butter (or hard margarine)	1/2 cup	125 mL
Egg yolks (large)	2	2
Whipping cream	1 cup	250 mL
Sliced fresh strawberries	3 cups	750 mL
Icing (confectioner's) sugar	1/4 cup	60 mL

Line bottom and side of greased 9 inch (22 cm) springform pan with parchment (not waxed) paper. Process cookies in blender or food processor until coarse crumbs. Transfer to medium bowl. Add liqueur. Stir. Let stand for 10 minutes.

Heat chocolate and butter in medium heavy saucepan on lowest heat, stirring often, until chocolate is almost melted. Do not overheat. Remove from heat. Stir until smooth.

Add egg yolks, 1 at a time, stirring well after each addition. Cool.

Beat whipping cream in small bowl until soft peaks form. Fold into chocolate mixture. Spread 1/3 of whipped cream mixture in prepared pan. Carefully sprinkle with half of cookie mixture, patting crumbs down lightly. Spread with half of remaining whipped cream mixture. Sprinkle with remaining cookie mixture. Pat crumbs down lightly. Carefully spread remaining whipped cream mixture evenly over top. Chill, covered, for at least 6 hours or overnight until set.

Arrange strawberries on top. Sprinkle with icing sugar. Cuts into 10 wedges.

1 wedge: 670 Calories; 45.7 g Total Fat (13.4 g Mono, 1.7 g Poly, 28.2 g Sat); 123 mg Cholesterol; 67 g Carbohydrate; 5 g Fibre; 5 g Protein; 206 mg Sodium

bocconne dolce

Chocolate, strawberries and cream smother meringue layers in this Italian dessert, pronounced boh-KOHN-nee DOHL-chay.

MERINGUE

Egg whites (large), room temperature	6	6
Cream of tartar	1/4 tsp.	1 mL
Granulated sugar	1 1/2 cups	375 mL

FILLING

Semi-sweet chocolate chips	1 cup	250 mL
Water	3 tbsp.	50 mL
Whipping cream	3 cups	750 mL
Granulated sugar	1/3 cup	75 mL
Vanilla extract	2 tsp.	10 mL
Fresh strawberries, sliced lengthwise	3 cups	750 mL

Fresh strawberries,
   for garnish
Chocolate curls
   (see Tip, page 64),
   for garnish

Meringue: Beat egg whites and cream of tartar in medium bowl until soft peaks form. Add sugar, 1 tbsp. (15 mL) at a time, beating constantly, until stiff peaks form and sugar is dissolved. Line bottoms of 2 baking sheets with parchment (not waxed) paper. Trace two 8 inch (20 cm) circles, about 1 1/2 inches (3.8 cm) apart, on first paper, and one 8 inch (20 cm) circle on second paper. Turn papers over (or use foil with circles marked on top). Spoon meringue onto circles. Spread evenly to edge of each. Bake in 250°F (120°C) oven for about 45 minutes until dry. Turn oven off. Let stand in oven with door ajar until cool. Remove meringues to wire racks and discard parchment paper.

Filling: Heat chocolate chips and water in small heavy saucepan on lowest heat, stirring often, until chips are almost melted. Do not overheat. Remove from heat. Stir until smooth. Spread over 2 meringues.

Beat next 3 ingredients in large bowl until soft peaks form. Spread over all 3 meringues.

Carefully place 1 meringue with chocolate filling on serving plate. Spoon half of sliced strawberries evenly over whipped cream. Place second meringue with chocolate filling on top. Spoon remaining strawberries evenly over whipped cream. Place third meringue on top.

Garnish with strawberries and chocolate curls. Chill for at least 6 hours or overnight. Serves 8.

1 serving: 612 Calories; 37.2 g Total Fat (11.1 g Mono, 1.3 g Poly, 22.9 g Sat); 110 mg Cholesterol; 70 g Carbohydrate; 3 g Fibre; 6 g Protein; 78 mg Sodium

grilled cake and strawberries

Lemon zest adds a nice balance to sweet grilled cake topped with strawberries and cream. Looks good—tastes heavenly!

Maple (or maple-flavoured) syrup	1/2 cup	125 mL
Orange juice	1/3 cup	75 mL
Hard margarine (or butter), melted	2 tbsp.	30 mL
Grated lemon zest	1 tsp.	5 mL
Frozen pound cake, thawed and crust removed	10 1/2 oz.	298 g
LEMON TOPPING		
Lemon spread (or curd)	1/2 cup	125 mL
Whipping cream	2 tbsp.	30 mL
Halved (or quartered, if large) fresh strawberries	3 cups	750 mL

Combine first 4 ingredients in small bowl.

Cut cake crosswise into 6 equal slices. Cut each slice in half diagonally, for a total of 12 pieces. Dip both sides of each piece into maple syrup mixture. Preheat gas barbecue to medium. Cook cake on greased grill for about 3 minutes per side until grill marks appear. Place 2 cake slices on each of 6 dessert plates.

Lemon Topping: Combine lemon spread and whipping cream in small saucepan on medium. Heat and stir for about 3 minutes until lemon spread is melted. Remove from heat. Let stand, uncovered, for 5 minutes.

Place strawberries in medium bowl. Drizzle with lemon spread mixture. Toss gently. Makes about 3 cups (750 mL) topping. Spoon about 1/2 cup (125 mL) topping on individual servings. Serves 6.

1 serving: 376 Calories; 15.2 g Total Fat (8.1 g Mono, 1.7 g Poly, 4.4 g Sat); 36 mg Cholesterol; 58 g Carbohydrate; 2 g Fibre; 4 g Protein; 319 mg Sodium

white chocolate mousse cake

Two cups of whole wafers crush to the amount needed for this fun, make-ahead dessert.

CRUST

Butter (or hard margarine)	1/3 cup	75 mL
Finely crushed vanilla wafers	1 1/4 cups	300 mL

FILLING

Envelope of unflavoured gelatin	1/4 oz.	7 g
Water	1/3 cup	75 mL
Block of cream cheese, softened	8 oz.	250 g
Granulated sugar	1/2 cup	125 mL
White chocolate bar, melted	6 oz.	170 g
Egg whites (large), room temperature	2	2
Whipping cream	1 cup	250 mL
Strawberry ice cream topping, large pieces chopped	1/3 cup	75 mL
Drop of red liquid food colouring	1	1

TOPPING

Fresh medium strawberries, hulled and halved lengthwise	26	26
Cranberry cocktail	1/2 cup	125 mL
Grenadine syrup	2 tbsp.	30 mL
Unflavoured gelatin	1 tsp.	5 mL

Crust: Melt butter in small saucepan on medium. Remove from heat. Add wafer crumbs. Mix well. Press firmly into bottom of ungreased 9 inch (22 cm) springform pan. Chill for 1 hour.

Filling: Sprinkle gelatin over water in small saucepan. Let stand for 1 minute. Heat and stir on low until gelatin is dissolved. Cool.

Beat cream cheese and sugar in large bowl until smooth. Add chocolate. Beat well. Add gelatin mixture. Beat well.

Beat egg whites with clean beaters in medium bowl until soft peaks form. Fold into cream cheese mixture.

Beat whipping cream in separate medium bowl until soft peaks form. Fold into cream cheese mixture. Makes about 3 3/4 cups (925 mL) filling. Reserve 1 1/2 cups (375 mL) in small bowl. Spoon remaining filling onto crust. Spread evenly.

Add ice cream topping and food colouring to reserved filling. Mix well. Spoon into piping bag fitted with 1/3 inch (1 cm) plain tip. Poke tip into filling in pan. Squeeze bag gently to squirt some filling into cake (inset photo). Repeat randomly all over with remaining strawberry mixture. Chill, covered, for at least 6 hours or overnight.

Topping: Arrange strawberries, cut-side down, in single layer on cake.

Combine cranberry cocktail and grenadine in small saucepan. Sprinkle gelatin over top. Let stand for 1 minute. Heat and stir on low until gelatin is dissolved. Cool to room temperature. Stir. Carefully pour over strawberries to cover completely. Chill for at least 6 hours or overnight. Cuts into 12 wedges.

1 wedge: 413 Calories; 26 g Total Fat (7.8 g Mono, 1.4 g Poly, 15.1 g Sat); 73 mg Cholesterol; 42 g Carbohydrate; 1 g Fibre; 5 g Protein; 196 mg Sodium

strawberry cream dessert

Very strawberry! A pretty ending to a meal.

CRUST

Butter (or hard margarine)	1/2 cup	125 mL
Graham cracker crumbs	2 cups	500 mL
Brown sugar, packed	1/4 cup	60 mL

FILLING

Reserved syrup from strawberries		
Box of strawberry jelly powder (gelatin)	3 oz.	85 g
Granulated sugar	1/2 cup	125 mL
Lemon juice	2 tbsp.	30 mL
Container of frozen strawberries in light syrup, thawed, drained and syrup reserved	15 oz.	425 g
Whipping cream	1 cup	250 mL

TOPPING

Whipping cream	1 cup	250 mL
Granulated sugar	2 tsp.	10 mL
Vanilla extract	1/2 tsp.	2 mL

Crust: Melt butter in small saucepan on medium. Remove from heat. Add graham crumbs and brown sugar. Mix well. Reserve 1/2 cup (125 mL) for topping. Press remaining crumbs firmly into ungreased 9 x 9 inch (22 x 22 cm) pan. Bake in 350°F (175°C) oven for 10 minutes. Let stand in pan on wire rack until cooled completely.

Filling: Heat syrup in small saucepan on medium. Add jelly powder and sugar. Stir until dissolved.

Add lemon juice. Stir. Cool for 10 minutes. Add strawberries. Stir. Chill, uncovered, for about 30 minutes until mixture starts to thicken.

Beat whipping cream in small bowl until soft peaks form. Fold into strawberry mixture. Pour over crust. Chill until set.

Topping: Beat first 3 ingredients in small bowl until soft peaks form. Spread over filling. Sprinkle with reserved graham crumb mixture. Chill. Cuts into 9 pieces.

1 piece: 470 Calories; 30.5 Total Fat (8.8 g Mono, 1.7 g Poly, 18.2 g Sat); 95 mg Cholesterol; 48 g Carbohydrate; 1 g Fibre; 4 g Protein; 246 mg Sodium

strawberry pizza pie

Beautiful fruit topping on a cake crust. The jelly "polishes" the fruit and prevents it from drying out.

CRUST

Hard margarine (or butter), softened	1/4 cup	60 mL
Brown sugar, packed	1/4 cup	60 mL
Granulated sugar	1/4 cup	60 mL
Large egg	1	1
Milk	1/4 cup	60 mL
Vanilla extract	1/2 tsp.	2 mL
All-purpose flour	1 3/4 cups	425 mL
Cream of tartar	1 tsp.	5 mL
Baking soda	1/2 tsp.	2 mL
Salt	1/4 tsp.	1 mL

FILLING

Block of cream cheese, softened	8 oz.	250 g
Icing (confectioner's) sugar	1 1/4 cups	300 mL
Lemon juice	1 tsp.	5 mL
Frozen whipped topping, thawed	2 cups	500 mL
Sliced fresh strawberries	2 1/2 cups	625 mL
Sliced kiwifruit	1 cup	250 mL

GLAZE

Apple jelly	1/3 cup	75 mL

Crust: Cream first 3 ingredients in medium bowl. Add next 3 ingredients. Beat well.

Combine next 4 ingredients in small bowl. Add to margarine mixture in 2 additions, mixing well after each addition until no dry flour remains. Press into greased 12 inch (30 cm) pizza pan. Bake in 375°F (190°C) oven for about 20 minutes until golden. Let stand in pan on wire rack until cooled completely.

Filling: Beat first 3 ingredients in medium bowl until light and fluffy. Fold in whipped topping. Spread evenly over crust.

Arrange strawberries and kiwifruit over cream cheese mixture.

Glaze: Heat jelly in small saucepan on medium-low, stirring occasionally, until melted. Brush lightly over fruit. Chill. Cuts into 10 wedges.

1 wedge: 440 Calories; 18.7 g Total Fat (6.1 g Mono, 1.1 g Poly, 10.2 g Sat); 49 mg Cholesterol; 64 g Carbohydrate; 3 g Fibre; 6 g Protein; 277 mg Sodium

berry pie

For a tarter flavour, add 1/4 cup (60 mL) more cranberries.

CRUST

All-purpose flour	1 3/4 cups	425 mL
Icing (confectioner's) sugar	3 tbsp.	50 mL
Baking powder	1/2 tsp.	2 mL
Cold butter (or hard margarine), cut up	1/2 cup	125 mL
Large egg, fork-beaten	1	1
Egg yolk (large), fork-beaten	1	1
Lemon juice, approximately	2 tbsp.	30 mL

FILLING

Sliced fresh strawberries	4 cups	1 L
Chopped fresh (or frozen, thawed) cranberries	1 cup	250 mL
Granulated sugar	1 cup	250 mL
Cornstarch	1/4 cup	60 mL
Ground cinnamon	1/2 tsp.	2 mL
Salt	1/4 tsp.	1 mL

TOPPING

Egg white (large), fork-beaten	1	1
Sanding (decorating) sugar (see Tip, page 64)	2 tsp.	10 mL

Crust: Combine first 3 ingredients in large bowl. Cut in butter until mixture resembles coarse crumbs.

Add egg and egg yolk. Stir, adding just enough lemon juice until soft dough forms. Divide pastry into 2 portions, making 1 portion slightly larger than the other. Shape each portion into slightly flattened disc. Roll out larger portion on lightly floured surface to about 1/8 inch (3 mm) thickness. Line 9 inch (22 cm) pie plate. Trim, leaving 1/2 inch (12 mm) overhang. Chill, covered, for 1 hour. Roll out smaller portion of pastry on lightly floured surface to 9 x 11 inch (22 x 28 cm) rectangle. Cut into eleven 3/4 inch (2 cm) strips with fluted pastry cutter. Place on baking sheet. Chill, covered, until ready to use.

Filling: Combine all 6 ingredients in large bowl. Spoon into pie shell. Spread evenly. Dampen edge of shell and both ends of pastry strips with water. Place 6 strips, side-by-side, equally spaced apart, on top of filling. Fold back 3 alternate strips to centre. Lay 1 strip across 3 remaining flat strips at centre. Return folded strips to flat position. Repeat, folding back 3 other alternate strips and laying 1 strip across flat strips. Repeat process, working from centre outward until all strips are woven into pie top. Trim strips at crust edge, leaving 1 inch (2.5 cm) overhang. Moisten and tuck strip ends under crust. Crimp decorative edge to seal.

Topping: Brush pastry with egg white. Sprinkle with sanding sugar. Bake on bottom rack in 375°F (190°C) oven for 50 to 55 minutes until pastry is golden and filling is bubbling. Cuts into 8 wedges.

1 wedge: 440 Calories; 18.7 g Total Fat (6.1 g Mono, 1.1 g Poly, 10.2 g Sat); 49 mg Cholesterol; 64 g Carbohydrate; 3 g Fibre; 6 g Protein; 277 mg Sodium

strawberry custard pie

This luscious pie can be made the day before, so it has plenty of time to set and you can check one thing off your entertaining to-do list.

Sliced almonds, toasted (see Tip, page 64)	1/2 cup	125 mL
Baked 9 inch (22 cm) pie shell	1	1
Boxes of instant vanilla pudding powder (4-serving size, each)	2	2
Milk	2 cups	500 mL
Frozen whipped topping, thawed	1 cup	250 mL
Sliced fresh strawberries	1 1/2 cups	375 mL
STRAWBERRY TOPPING		
Mashed (or puréed) strawberries	1/2 cup	125 mL
Water	1/2 cup	125 mL
Granulated sugar	1/4 cup	60 mL
Cornstarch	1 tbsp.	15 mL

Scatter almonds in pie shell.

Beat pudding powder and milk in large bowl until smooth. Fold in whipped topping. Pour over almonds. Chill for 1 hour.

Arrange strawberries over top of pie.

Strawberry Topping: Combine all 4 ingredients in small heavy saucepan. Heat and stir on medium-high until boiling and thickened. Cool completely. Spoon over strawberries. Chill, covered, for at least 6 hours or overnight. Cuts into 8 wedges.

1 wedge: 347 Calories; 14.1 g Total Fat (6.2 g Mono, 2.5 g Poly, 4.8 g Sat); 3 mg Cholesterol; 52 g Carbohydrate; 1 g Fibre; 5 g Protein; 249 mg Sodium

fresh strawberry pie

What a showpiece! Check around for the reddest, freshest strawberries. Real whipping cream also works well.

Fresh whole strawberries	5 cups	1.25 L
Baked 9 inch (22 cm) pie shell	1	1
Water	1 2/3 cups	400 mL
Granulated sugar	1 cup	250 mL
Drops of red liquid food colouring (optional)	6	6
Water	1/3 cup	75 mL
Cornstarch	3 tbsp.	50 mL
Box of strawberry jelly powder (gelatin)	3 oz.	85 g

TOPPING

Frozen whipped topping, thawed	1 cup	250 mL
Sliced fresh strawberries, for garnish		

Arrange strawberries, pointed ends up, in pie shell.

Combine first amount of water and sugar in small heavy saucepan. Add food colouring. Heat and stir on medium-high until boiling.

Stir second amount of water into cornstarch in small cup. Add to sugar mixture. Heat and stir until boiling and thickened. Remove from heat.

Add jelly powder. Stir until dissolved. Cool completely. Carefully spoon over berries. Chill until set.

Topping: Spread whipped topping over top. Garnish with strawberries. Cuts into 8 wedges.

1 wedge: 355 Calories; 12.9 g Total Fat (5.5 g Mono, 2.6 g Poly, 8.3 g Sat); 0 mg Cholesterol; 59 g Carbohydrate; 1 g Fibre; 3 g Protein; 174 mg Sodium

recipe index

topical tips

Curling chocolate: To make chocolate curls, peel room temperature chocolate firmly along its length with a sharp vegetable peeler.

Making soured milk: If a recipe calls for sour milk, measure 1 tbsp. (15 mL) white vinegar or lemon juice into a 1 cup (250 mL) liquid measure. Add enough milk to make 1 cup (250 mL). Stir. Let stand for 1 minute.

Sanding (decorating) sugar: Sanding sugar is a coarse decorating sugar that comes in white and various colours and is available at specialty kitchen stores.

Toasting nuts, seeds or coconut: Cooking times will vary for each type of nut, so never toast them together. For small amounts, place ingredient in an ungreased shallow frying pan. Heat on medium for three to five minutes, stirring often, until golden. For larger amounts, spread ingredient evenly in an ungreased shallow pan. Bake in a 350°F (175°C) oven for five to 10 minutes, stirring or shaking often, until golden.

Nutrition Information Guidelines

Each recipe is analyzed using the Canadian Nutrient File from Health Canada, which is based on the United States Department of Agriculture (USDA) Nutrient Database.

- If more than one ingredient is listed (such as "butter or hard margarine"), or if a range is given (1 – 2 tsp., 5 – 10 mL), only the first ingredient or first amount is analyzed.

- For meat, poultry and fish, the serving size per person is based on the recommended 4 oz. (113 g) uncooked weight (without bone), which is 2 – 3 oz. (57 – 85 g) cooked weight (without bone)— approximately the size of a deck of playing cards.

- Milk used is 1% M.F. (milk fat), unless otherwise stated.

- Cooking oil used is canola oil, unless otherwise stated.

- Ingredients indicating "sprinkle," "optional," or "for garnish" are not included in the nutrition information.

- The fat in recipes and combination foods can vary greatly depending on the sources and types of fats used in each specific ingredient. For these reasons, the count of saturated, monounsaturated and polyunsaturated fats may not add up to the total fat content.